*"If ever this vast country is bro
ment, it will be one of the most extensive corruptions."*
—Thomas Jefferson, 1822

Thomas Jefferson

"Enemy of Statism"

"Friend of Liberty"

*"I would rather be exposed to the inconveniences attending
too much liberty, than those attending too small a degree of it."*
—Thomas Jefferson, 1791

*"The God who gave us life, gave us liberty at the same time:
the hand of force may destroy, but cannot disjoin them."*
—Thomas Jefferson, 1808

About the "Uncle Eric" Series

The "Uncle Eric" series of books is written by Richard J. Maybury for young and old alike. Using the epistolary style of writing (using letters to tell a story), Mr. Maybury plays the part of an economist writing a series of letters to his niece or nephew. Using stories and examples, he gives interesting and clear explanations of topics that are generally thought to be too difficult for anyone but experts.

Mr. Maybury warns, "beware of anyone who tells you a topic is above you or better left to experts. Many people are twice as smart as they think they are but they've been intimidated into believing some topics are above them. You can understand almost anything if it is explained well."

The series is called UNCLE ERIC'S MODEL OF HOW THE WORLD WORKS. Each book in the series attempts to be consistent with the principles of America's Founders. The books can be read in any order, and have been written to stand alone. To get the most from each one, however, here is Mr. Maybury's suggested order of reading.

Uncle Eric's Model of How the World Works

Book 1. UNCLE ERIC TALKS ABOUT PERSONAL, CAREER AND FINANCIAL SECURITY. Uncle Eric's Model introduced.

Book 2. WHATEVER HAPPENED TO PENNY CANDY?
The economic model explained.

Book 3. WHATEVER HAPPENED TO JUSTICE?
The legal model explained. Explores America's legal heritage.

Book 4. ARE YOU LIBERAL? CONSERVATIVE? OR CONFUSED?
Political labels. What do they mean?

Book 5. ANCIENT ROME: HOW IT AFFECTS YOU TODAY.
Mr. Maybury uses historical events to explain current events.

Book 6. EVALUATING BOOKS: WHAT WOULD THOMAS JEFFERSON THINK ABOUT THIS? Learn how to identify the philosophical slant of most writers and media commentators on the subjects of law, economics, and history.

Evaluating Books

What Would Thomas Jefferson Think About This?

**Guidelines for Selecting Books
Consistent with the
Principles of America's Founders**

**by Richard J. Maybury
("Uncle Eric")**

published by
Bluestocking Press
P.O. Box 1014 • Dept. EB
Placerville • CA • 95667-1014

Printed in the United States of America.

Edited by Jane A. Williams.

Cover graphic used with permission: Copyrighted by the White House Historical Association; Photograph by the National Geographic Society.

Thomas Jefferson, page 1, Painting by Rembrandt Peale. Courtesy Princeton University. Reproduced from the *Dictionary of American Portraits*, published by Dover Publications, Inc., 1967. Thomas Jefferson, profile graphic which faces quotes throughout book: Painting attributed to James Sharples, Sr. Courtesy Independence National Historical Park. Reproduced from the *Dictionary of American Portraits*, published by Dover Publications, Inc., 1967.

Library of Congress Cataloging-in-Publication Data
Maybury, Rick.
    Evaluating books : what would Thomas Jefferson think about
  this? : guidelines for selecting books consistent with the principles
  of America's founders / by Richard J. Maybury   (Uncle Eric) .
        p.   cm. -- (An "Uncle Eric" book)
    Includes bibliographical references and index.
    ISBN 0-942617-14-2 : $8.95
    1. Books and reading--United States.   2. Libertarianism--
  United States.   I. Title.   II. Series: Maybury, Rick.   "Uncle
  Eric" book.
  Z1003.2.M38   1994
  028.5--dc20   93-5078
                                                                        CIP

Published by   **Bluestocking Press**
                        Post Office Box 1014
                              Dept. EB
                    Placerville, CA 95667-1014

To M,
my closest friend and one of the finest people
I've ever known. She taught me compassion,
and changed me in a hundred ways. I miss her.

Contents

How to Use This Book

The "Uncle Eric" books are a series. Each book builds on those that come before it. Although each can stand alone, it will be clearer and more helpful if you read the series in this order: 1) WHATEVER HAPPENED TO PENNY CANDY? 2) WHATEVER HAPPENED TO JUSTICE? and 3) EVALUATING BOOKS: WHAT WOULD THOMAS JEFFERSON THINK ABOUT THIS?

WHATEVER HAPPENED TO PENNY CANDY? explains economics. WHATEVER HAPPENED TO JUSTICE? explains law and the connection between law and economics.

A good way to use this book is to read it twice. First go through it cover to cover underlining points most important to you. Also make a list of the recommended books and other publications you'll want to get.

After you've read these, reread this book and refer back to the others wherever appropriate. This will give you all the background you need to confidently select books consistent with the principles on which America was founded.

**What Would
Thomas Jefferson
Think About This?**

"Only lay down true principles, and adhere to them inflexibly."
—Thomas Jefferson, 1816

Evaluating Books

Dear Reader,

My purpose here is to help you avoid books that teach misleading or harmful information, especially information that is contrary to basic American principles described in the writings of Thomas Jefferson and the other American founders.

My focus is on political power. As explained in WHATEVER HAPPENED TO JUSTICE?[1] political power is the privilege of using force on persons who have not harmed anyone. This is what sets government apart from businesses, churches, charities and other private organizations. No private organization can legally send men with guns to your home to force you to obey its wishes.[2]

> *"It will be of little avail to the people that the laws are made by men of their own choice if the laws be so voluminous that they cannot be read, or so incoherent that they cannot be understood."*
>
> — James Madison, 1787

---

[1] WHATEVER HAPPENED TO JUSTICE? by Richard J. Maybury, published by Bluestocking Press, Placerville, CA. 1993.

[2] For those who believe it can't happen here, I recommend you read MANZANAR by John Armor and Peter Wright, published by Vintage, a division of Random House.

The coercive nature of political power is why America's founders believed this power is inherently evil, it corrupts. They were trying to set up a government which would have extremely limited power so that it would not be able to do much damage.

The founders were convinced that governments are, fundamentally, predators. These predators must be kept small and weak or they will destroy law and devour the country.

What Would Thomas Jefferson Think About This?

"I think we have more machinery of government than is necessary, too many parasites living on the labor of the industries."
— Thomas Jefferson, 1824

Jefferson wrote these words when the federal government had only about 8,500 civilian employees; today it has more than three million.

The prevailing political viewpoints today are the opposite of the original American philosophy. They contend that political power is wonderful stuff and everyone should have some. Government is our friend, our protector, the solution to our problems, they say.

These prevailing philosophies can be grouped under the label "statism." Statists advocate the use of political power to achieve whatever they think necessary.

Many statists believe political power is a fine and necessary tool for reorganizing the economy, meaning for reorganizing your work, production and trade — they wish to control you by force.

Schoolbooks are saturated with statism. This is not to say textbook writers have formed a conspiracy to brainwash students. In most cases the writers do not know they are teaching concepts that are the opposite of the original American philosophy. They teach only what they were taught.

Rarely will you find a book that adheres 100% to the original American philosophy, which I introduced in WHAT-EVER HAPPENED TO JUSTICE? So, parents, your children will be exposed to statism—to power lust. You will need to decide how much exposure you want them to have. The more they know about the original American philosophy and economics, the more statism they can read without being seriously misled.

What Would Thomas Jefferson Think About This?

"Reading, reflection and time have convinced me that the interests of society require the observation of those moral precepts only in which all religions agree (for all forbid us to murder, steal, plunder, or bear false witness) ... The varieties in structure and action of the human mind as in those of the body, are the work of our Creator, against which it cannot be a religious duty to erect the standard of uniformity."
—Thomas Jefferson, 1809

A good way to judge how ready they are is to ask them to argue both sides of a variety of issues. From newspapers or TV select stories that raise questions about law, government, economics or foreign policy. You or someone else take the pro-liberty side and the child takes the statist side. Then midway through the debate, at a time of your choosing, suddenly switch sides. Then switch back, and back again.

The child should be persuasive on either side. This indicates the deep knowledge you are seeking.

Some books that will help you with this are the "Opposing Viewpoints" series published by Greenhaven Press, and the "Evaluating Viewpoints—Critical Thinking in United States History" series published by Critical Thinking Press and Software. Don't use them blindly. Use the source documents to help with your debates but be alert to the editorializing that accompanies the source documents.

But, you ask, if the child knows that much about statism, doesn't this run the risk that he or she will be seduced by the statist side?

No. You know your child. Is he dedicated to Higher Law, meaning the two fundamental laws explained in WHATEVER HAPPENED TO JUSTICE?[3] If yes, you have nothing to worry about.

If the child is dedicated to Higher Law and can argue both sides of a variety of issues, he or she can be safely exposed to any statist literature. For sources of books and other materials that adhere closely to American principles see pages 101 and 102 of this book.

---

[3]For a further explanation of the two fundamental laws, refer to the articles that begin on page 86 *(A Tribute to the Statue of Ellis Island)* and page 91 *(The Founding Fathers: Smugglers, Tax Evaders and Traitors)*, as well as the book WHATEVER HAPPENED TO JUSTICE? published by Bluestocking Press.

To judge a book I suggest you use a point system. Add points for each mention of the costs or dangers of political power, and subtract points for anything that legitimizes political power. The higher the score the better the book.

Bear in mind that statist viewpoints are seldom voiced outright. Often they are presented subtly, readers are led to jump to conclusions that are not true.

Also remember that our reading of history forms our attitudes. We make decisions on the basis of what we believe worked or didn't work in the past. So, he who controls the slant of the history books controls our thoughts and therefore our actions. This is the most important reason for parents and guardians to screen the books children read. To fail to screen is to leave the child's mind, and his future, in the hands of persons who have never met him and may care nothing about him. These persons may even have a hidden agenda that includes using the child as an expendable pawn.

The books and audiocassettes listed in the "Recommended Reading and Listening" sections throughout this book have been selected because they tend to be politically consistent with original American principles, but this is not meant to be a blanket endorsement of these resources. Parental discretion is always advised.

For an excellent — and frightening — example of what *not* to teach your children, read the two highly acclaimed books by historian Howard Zinn, A PEOPLE'S HISTORY OF THE UNITED STATES and DECLARATIONS OF INDEPENDENCE (both published by Harper Collins). These are cleverly disguised statism. They attempt to discredit virtually everything America stands for. Expose your child to them only *after* he or she has a good background in free-market economics, common law and the beliefs of America's founders. Such books receive rave reviews because few reviewers have this background.

Author Zinn advocates overthrow of the existing order in America — which by itself is not necessarily a bad idea — but what do we replace it with? Zinn ridicules common law and free markets, so the system of liberty is out, according to him.

He does give a vague description of a new order of "co-operation" but his plan is so lacking in specifics that it would surely lead to chaos. Remember what happened in Yugoslavia in 1991 when the existing order was overthrown without anyone having a clear notion of a workable alternative.

Until the collapse of the Soviet Union, most statists advocated overthrow of the existing order in the United States and replacement with socialism. But the clear failure of the socialist economies now leaves statists with no new plan. Zinn's suggestion, which is representative of those popular now, seems to be a kind of utopia. He writes,

> "Everyone could share the routine but necessary jobs for a few hours a day, and leave most of the time free for enjoyment, creativity, labors of love, and yet produce enough for an equal and ample distribution of goods. Certain basic things would be abundant enough to be taken out of the money system and be available —free—to everyone: food, housing, health care, education, transportation."

No kidding, that's what this eminent historian promises, free lunches.

Statist books usually do expose many hidden and unpleasant truths, which is why they can be so persuasive to young minds that have been fed only whitewash all their lives.

Zinn's work is an excellent example, it drags many skeletons out of the American closet, which is good but.... These skeletons really amount to no more than proof that America's founders didn't get it all perfect on the first try. Someone who comes to these statist works unprepared can be terribly shaken by them.

Statist books should be an integral part of your child's learning *after* the child is thoroughly grounded in the legal and economic principles on which America was founded.

You won't have any trouble finding statist works. Use the history, economics and political science books on the approved textbook lists for almost any public school system.

Beginning on page 18 are some Negative Indicators — statist viewpoints and half-truths—to watch for. On pages 54-57 are Misleading Terms. Positive Indicators are listed on pages 59-80. But first, I'll answer a question some of you might be asking — "just who were America's Founders, and why the emphasis on Thomas Jefferson?"

Richard J. Maybury
("Uncle Eric")

The American Founders

The American Revolution was in two parts. The first was the war surrounding the 1776 Declaration of Independence. The second was the creation of the 1787 Constitution and 1791 Bill of Rights.

Any prominent person who was influential in either of these parts and who was in general or exact agreement with the principles described in my book WHATEVER HAPPENED TO JUSTICE? should be called an American founder. I could list hundreds, but the twelve founders listed on page seventeen are the most well known.

Jefferson and Paine were probably the most important— they gave guidance by articulating the principles. Not that others didn't give guidance, but Jefferson and Paine gave the most.

Unfortunately, this guidance has been almost entirely erased from American culture and American history. Few Americans today know anything about the principles of the founders; history has become little more than a list of names, dates and wars. I urge you to read the works of the founders, you will find them most enlightening.

"In a recent survey, new college graduates listed history as the academic subject whose lessons they found of least use in their daily lives."

William Straus & Neil Howe
GENERATIONS, 1991

America's Founders

John Adams	John Jay
Samuel Adams	Thomas Jefferson
Benjamin Franklin	James Madison
Alexander Hamilton	George Mason
John Hancock	Thomas Paine
Patrick Henry	George Washington

Recommended Listening

COMMON SENSE, THOMAS PAINE, THE DECLARATION OF INDEPENDENCE, THOMAS JEFFERSON; THE WEALTH OF NATIONS, ADAM SMITH; THE FEDERALIST PAPERS, ALEXANDER HAMILTON, JAMES MADISON, JOHN JAY; TWO TREATISES ON GOVERNMENT, JOHN LOCKE; DEMOCRACY IN AMERICA, ALEXIS DE TOCQUEVILLE (from *Giants of Political Thought* series). Also, *United States Constitution* series, including: THE CONSTITUTIONAL CONVENTION, THE RATIFICATION DEBATES, THE TEXT OF THE U.S. CONSTITUTION, THE BILL OF RIGHTS AND ADDITIONAL AMENDMENTS. Both series produced by Knowledge Products, Nashville, TN, distributed by Bluestocking Press. For ages 14+.

Negative Indicators

The General Statist Viewpoint

Political power is good and everyone should have lots of it. Its benefits are greater than its costs, and it can solve our problems. This is the unspoken statist viewpoint found in virtually all school books published today.

The Other Side of the Story

A book can be factual without being truthful. A clever writer can make any viewpoint sound plausible simply by presenting facts that support the viewpoint and omitting facts that refute it. His presentation will be factual but misleading.[4]

What I attempt to do in my books is present the omitted facts—the other side of the story—the way I believe America's founders would want these facts presented. The Founders hated political power, were afraid of it, and believed

---

[4]Here are three books written to give the side of the story that is usually absent from literature our children usually study: FACTS THE HISTORIANS LEAVE OUT and WAR FOR WHAT? by Francis W. Springer, published by Bill Coats Ltd., Tennessee (about the War Between the States) and THROUGH INDIAN EYES: THE NATIVE EXPERIENCE IN BOOKS FOR CHILDREN by Beverly Slapin and Doris Seale, published by New Society Publishers, Philadelphia, PA.

it is fundamentally evil. They believed the only "real world" solution is to keep power widely dispersed and so limited that no one has much interest in it—it's virtually irrelevant.

What Would Thomas Jefferson Think About This?

"...a wise and frugal government, which shall restrain men from injuring one another, which shall leave them otherwise free to regulate their own pursuits of industry and improvement, and shall not take from the mouth of labor the bread it has earned. This is the sum of good government."
—Thomas Jefferson, 1801

"Sometimes it is said that man cannot be trusted with the government of himself. Can he, then, be trusted with the government of others?"
— Thomas Jefferson, 1801

The following pages include specific issues giving the statist viewpoint and "other side of the story."

Issue #1

The Great Depression

Statist Viewpoint

The Great Depression was caused by a failure of capitalism or free enterprise.

The Other Side of the Story

The Great Depression was caused by the Federal Reserve. In the 1920s, officials inflated the currency and thereby caused massive amounts of malinvestment.

Malinvestment is mistaken investment. Investment is the production of factories, office buildings, machinery and other *tools* necessary to create jobs. Malinvestment is the formation of these tools in locations or ways that are not viable when the money supply stops expanding.

> "...All the perplexities, confusion and distress in America arise, not from the defects in their constitution or confederation, not from want of honor or virtue, so much as from downright ignorance of the nature of coin, credit and circulation..."
>
> John Quincy Adams, 1829

In other words, when the Federal Reserve injects money into the economy, this money distorts prices and profits. Firms are lured into making mistakes — malinvestments — that must be corrected. The correction period is a depression.

The 1920s inflation of the money supply led to the 1930s Great Depression which was the worst in US history.

What Would Thomas Jefferson Think About This?

"That paper money has some advantages, is admitted. But that its abuses also are inevitable, and, by breaking up the measure of value, makes a lottery of all private property, cannot be denied. Shall we ever be able to put a constitutional veto on it?"
— Thomas Jefferson, 1817

Recommended Reading

AMERICA'S GREAT DEPRESSION by Murray Rothbard. Published by Richardson & Snyder, NY, 1983. For ages 15 and up.

WHAT YOU SHOULD KNOW ABOUT INFLATION by Henry Hazlitt. Published by Funk & Wagnalls, NY, 1968. For ages 14 and up.

WHATEVER HAPPENED TO PENNY CANDY? by Richard J. Maybury. Published by Bluestocking Press, Placerville, CA. For ages 10 and up.

Issue #2

Franklin Roosevelt's New Deal

Statist Viewpoint

Franklin Roosevelt's New Deal ended the Great Depression.

The Other Side of the Story

The Japanese navy ended the Great Depression. The New Deal probably prolonged the depression by delaying correction of the malinvestments.

The government's own statistics on unemployment and production show clearly that the depression was still on in 1939, six years after the New Deal began.

When Pearl Harbor was bombed, the goverment had an excuse to inflate with wild abandon to pay for the war. This new money breathed new life into the malinvestment, much of which is still with us today.

Recommended Reading

HISTORICAL STATISTICS OF THE UNITED STATES, Bureau of the Census, Government Printing Office. See the unemployment, per capita, GNP and money supply statistics relating to the 1920s and 1930s.

Issue #3

Progressive Taxes

Statist Viewpoint

Progressive taxes are good. (Under a "progressive" tax, persons who earn more pay more.)

The Other Side of the Story

If "progressive" pricing of government services is good, why not progressive pricing of everything? If you earn twice as much as your neighbor, you pay twice as much for bread, shoes, housing, etc. Think about it.

Recommended Reading

ECONOMICS IN ONE LESSON (See Chapter 5) by Henry Hazlitt, Crown. Published by Crown, New York. For ages 15 and up.

What Would Thomas Jefferson Think About This?

"If we run into such [government] debts, as that we must be taxed in our meat and in our drink, in our necessaries and our comforts, in our labors and our amusements, for our callings and our creeds, as the people of England are, our people, like them, must come to labor sixteen hours in the twenty-four, give the earnings of fifteen of these to the government for their debts and daily expenses; and the sixteenth being insufficient to afford us bread, we must live, as they now do, on oatmeal and potatoes; have no time to think, no means of calling the mismanagers to account; but be glad to obtain subsistence by hiring ourselves to rivet their chains on the necks of our fellow-sufferers."
— Thomas Jefferson, 1816

Issue #4

Robber Baron Capitalists

Statist Viewpoint

Controls on business people became necessary during the late 1800s because "robber baron capitalists" were mistreating workers and charging unfair prices.

The Other Side of the Story

I urge you to read THE MYTH OF THE ROBBER BARONS by Burton W. Folsom, Jr. (1991, 170 pages, published by Young America's Foundation, 110 Elden St., Herndon, VA 22091.) American's are taught that the early industrialists were corrupt "robber barons" who charged unfair prices and wages until they were brought under control by the heroic United States government. Folsom correctly shows that there were two groups of early industrialists. One was the monopolists who were indeed corrupt and were able to commit unforgivable abuses because the government was helping them do so. The other was the market entrepreneurs who had little or no connection with government and behaved honorably, helping improve the lot of workers and consumers alike.

In the absence of government privileges and subsidies, the only controls that are necessary are those provided naturally through the principles of common law and the forces of competition.

What Would Thomas Jefferson Think About This?

"Agriculture, manufactures, commerce and navigation, the four pillars of our prosperity, are the most thriving when left the most free to individual enterprise."
— Thomas Jefferson, 1801

Recommended Reading

"ANTITRUST" by Alan Greenspan and "NOTES ON THE HISTORY OF AMERICAN FREE ENTERPRISE" by Ayn Rand, both in the book CAPITALISM: THE UNKNOWN IDEAL by Ayn Rand. Published by Signet, Times Mirror, NY, 1966, For ages 15 and up.

THE MYTH OF THE ROBBER BARONS by Burton W. Folsom, Jr. Published by Young America's Foundation, 110 Elden St., Herndon, VA 22091. For ages 14 and up.

Issue #5

Governments Aren't Greedy

Statist Viewpoint

Business people are motivated by greed and are not to be trusted. Government officials, on the other hand, are not greedy and can be trusted because they are selfless and motivated by a desire to protect and help us.

The Other Side of the Story

This viewpoint is rarely stated outright as I have done here, and you can see why. It's probably true that most people and organizations are motivated by greed to one extent or another, and it is abundantly true that governments are to a great extent. Every day your local newspaper is packed with announcements about businesses lowering their prices. When was the last time you got a break on your taxes?

Politicians and bureaucrats are as human as the rest of us and have all the same motivations and vices—except that they also have the privilege of satisfying their motivations and vices through the use of force.

What Would Thomas Jefferson Think About This?

"Offices are as acceptable here as elsewhere, and whenever a man has cast a longing eye on them, a rottenness begins in his conduct."
—Thomas Jefferson, 1799

Issue #6

Child Labor Laws

Statist Viewpoint

Child labor laws were enacted to protect children from mistreatment by employers. These laws are good and necessary.

The Other Side of the Story

The issue is too complex to fully explain here but we can mention two points. (For an in-depth study refer to the recommended readings on page 31.)

First, a child who is suffering from sexual abuse or some other mistreatment cannot easily escape today because he or she cannot earn a living. Those who do escape end up wandering the streets and surviving through prostitution, theft or other crime because they cannot get a legitimate job.

Second, the child labor laws have destroyed the apprentice system. Children cannot learn a trade and become independent as they did in past centuries. They are forced to remain children long past the age when their ancestors had become journeymen carpenters, mechanics and tailors.

This isn't to say the very young should not be protected, it is only to say statist writers accept the so-called benefits of child labor laws without question and without examining the *hidden* costs.

Alternative Solution

Many states permit children to own and operate their own businesses.

Recommended Reading

BETTER THAN A LEMONADE STAND! by fifteen-year-old Daryl Bernstein. Published by Beyond Words Publishing. For ages 10 and up.

CAPITALISM FOR KIDS: GROWING UP TO BE YOUR OWN BOSS by Karl Hess. Published by Enterprise Publishing. For ages 9 and up.

"THE EFFECT OF THE INDUSTRIAL REVOLUTION ON WOMEN AND CHILDREN" by Robert Hessen in CAPITALISM: THE UNKOWN IDEAL by Ayn Rand (Chapter 8). For ages 14 and up.

"THE SCHOOLS AIN'T WHAT THEY USED TO BE AND NEVER WAS" in THE LIBERTARIAN ALTERNATIVE by Tibor Machan (Chapter 15). Published by Nelson Hall, Chicago, 1977. For ages 16 and up.

THE TEENAGE ENTREPRENEUR'S GUIDE: 50 MONEY-MAKING BUSINESS IDEAS by Sarah L. Riehm. Published by Surrey Books. For ages 13 and up.

Issue #7

Farmers Had Happier Lives

Statist Viewpoint

Before the Industrial Revolution, life was better. People were happy and healthy living and working on farms. The industrial revolution locked them up in "dark satanic mills."

The Other Side of the Story

America is the only major nation that has never had a famine. The possibility of our children starving to death is so far outside the experience of most Americans that we have no comprehension of what life was like worldwide before 1776.

**What Would
Thomas Jefferson
Think About This?**

"I shall, therefore rejoin myself to my native country, with new attachments, and with exaggerated esteem for its advantages; for though there is less wealth there, there is more freedom, more ease, and less misery."

— Thomas Jefferson, 1785

(about his return to America from France)

The mills of the early Industrial Revolution were grim by today's standards, but they were a vast improvement over anything that came before, and they boosted production and reduced prices of clothing and other essentials. A mill worker didn't worry about starving or freezing to death as most other workers did. The happy, healthy farm worker of pre-industrial times did not exist. Most were forever hungry, dirty, flea ridden, diseased and barely a step ahead of the Grim Reaper.

George Washington was part of America's upper class. When he was in his early teens he wrote 110 *"Rules of Civility & Decent Behaviour in Company and Conversation"* into his copybook. Rule #13:

> "Kill no vermin as fleas, lice, ticks &c in the sight of others; if you see any filth or thick spittle, put your foot dexteriously upon it; if it be upon the clothes of your companions, put it off privately; and if it be upon your own clothes, return thanks to him who puts it off."

The early mills were no place a modern American would want to work but the fact is that in most cases they were the best that could be done at that time and they saved the lives of the men, women and children who worked there.

A book I dearly wish I could recommend is EVERYDAY LIFE THROUGH THE AGES (published by The Reader's Digest Association Limited, 1992). This beautifully illustrated and smoothly written volume is heavily researched and packed with fascinating information about the way humans lived in earlier times. This is history as it should be presented, with emphasis not on politics but on economics.

The books's fatal flaw is that much of its explanation of events has a strong statist slant echoing the myths commonly taught in schools and colleges throughout the United States. For instance on page 271 the books says, "Hardship and poverty were widespread side effects of the Industrial Revolution." On page 269 the book laments the ten-hour shifts worked by women in Scottish coal mines.

Yet five pages earlier it correctly reports that in pre-industrial times, "men, women and children of entire villages — even of whole country towns — would be out in the fields, often working 16 hour days, and by moonlight if necessary," and "it was painful work." The book quotes the son of a farmer saying, "no one could stand the harvest-field as a reaper except he had been born to it." On page 150 it correctly reports that "Death and disease were no strangers to the filth-ridden towns and villages of medieval Europe." Few lived till old-age and famine was common. On page 271, after decrying the Industrial Revolution, the book even admits that in one English town "only 100 of the 9000 inhabitants were fully employed." These people were so poor that "many fasted every other day, or survived on boiled nettles."

In other words, the truth is that hardship and poverty were not caused by the Industrial Revolution, they existed long before it; the Industrial Revolution was the cure.

If the mills of the early Industrial Revolution were so terrible, why did workers in every nation leave their farms, and flock to the cities to get jobs in these mills?

Recommended Reading

FACTS ABOUT THE INDUSTRIAL REVOLUTION by Ludwig von Mises in FREE MARKET ECONOMICS, A BASIC READER by Bettina Bien Greaves, published by the Foundation for Economic Education, Irvington-on-Hudson, NY. For ages 15 and up.

Issue #8

Poverty and Crime

Statist Viewpoint
Poverty breeds crime.

The Other Side of the Story
This is one of the most corrosive and misleading state-
ments in American culture today, and it's so pervasive it is
rarely questioned.

"Poverty breeds crime," says to every poor person, "because you have a low income you are automatically disposed
to being evil and brutal." How much hope can people have if
they are continually receiving this message? Will they work
hard to overcome their difficulties or will they just give up?

This viewpoint in particular is such a frustration because
it is so clearly false. If poverty bred crime, then the 1930s
Great Depression would have brought a crime wave of un-
imaginable proportions. Talk with anyone who remembers
those times. They are likely to tell you about the "good old
days" when they could leave their doors unlocked and safely
walk their neighborhood streets at any time of the day or night.

HISTORICAL STATISTICS OF THE UNITED STATES: COLONIAL
TIMES TO 1957, (U.S. Department of Commerce, 1961, pages

217 and 218) shows crime statistics indicating that the number of people going to prison during the Great Depression actually declined from previous years.

For all of history prior to this century, everyone lived in poverty so grim we can hardly imagine it. Even royalty. They were continually threatened by scurvy because they had no fresh fruits in the winter. They had no good dental care or medical care. Most were illiterate. They had no electric lights, no hot or cold running water or indoor plumbing; or eye glasses. In their wildest dreams they never imagined the "necessities" we take for granted: television, radio, telephones, computers, stereos, microwave ovens, refrigerators, central heating and air conditioning, cotton clothing, sunscreen lotion, automobiles and on and on.

And that was royalty.

Try to grasp how awful it was for the common folk. Few lived as well as America's poorest do today.

Were all our ancestors criminals?

The wealthy royal families were criminals. Their wealth was acquired by forcibly taking it from others.

Granted, in previous centuries there were certain areas that were bad. No sane person would have wanted to spend much time in central Paris, Dodge City or Port Royal, Jamaica for instance. But if poverty causes crime, then stealing and murder would have been the norm and civilization would have quickly collapsed long ago.

In 1940, teachers were surveyed about problems in the public schools. Compare their top problems with those cited by teachers in 1990:

1940 Public School Problems	1990 Public School Problems
Talking out of turn	Drug and alcohol abuse
Chewing gum	Pregnancy
Making noise	Suicide
Running in the halls	Rape
Cutting in line	Robbery
Dress code infractions	Assault[5]
Littering	

According to THE STATISTICAL ABSTRACT OF THE UNITED STATES, real (inflation-adjusted) median family income in 1990 was roughly three times that of 1940. So, why did the much poorer Americans of 1940 not have to worry about their children being raped, robbed or assaulted in school?

If poverty causes crime, the schools of 1940 should have been war zones and those of today should be utopias.

This isn't to say poverty is a fine thing, it's terrible, but it does not cause crime.

Crime is not about poverty it is about character. If there is crime in the poorer areas of our nation today, you can figure something is destroying the character of the people there.

> "According to our research crime is underestimated by about 600%....we were unprepared for the revelation that fully 60% or 600 in every 1000 adult Americans have been the victim of at least one crime....We further found that 350 in every 1000 Americans have been the victims of at least two crimes."
> —James Patterson and Peter Kim
> THE DAY AMERICA TOLD THE TRUTH

---

[5]CQ RESEARCHER, September 11, 1993.

Issue #9

Wage-and-Price Spiral

Statist Viewpoint
The wage-and-price spiral causes rising prices.

The Other Side of the Story
Rising prices are caused by inflation of the money supply.

Recommended Reading and Listening

THE INFLATION CRISIS AND HOW TO RESOLVE IT (formerly WHAT YOU SHOULD KNOW ABOUT INFLATION) by Henry Hazlitt. For order information contact The Foundation for Economic Education, Irvington-on-Hudson, NY. For ages 16 and up.

THE GREAT ECONOMIC THINKERS Knowledge Products audiocassette series, Nashville, TN. Ages 15+.

WHATEVER HAPPENED TO PENNY CANDY? 3rd edition, by Richard J. Maybury published by Bluestocking Press, 1993. For ages 10 and up.

Issue #10

Needs of Society

Statist Viewpoint

The needs of society outweigh the needs of the individual.

The Other Side of the Story

Whenever someone starts talking about the needs of society, look out. The whole is not greater than the sum of its parts.

Society has no needs, only individuals have needs. Remove all the individuals and there is no society.

Beware of all collectivist terminology — "national interests," "social concerns," "social goods," "community needs," "public services." These fuzzy but high sounding phrases diminish the importance of the individual and serve as excuses to place more power in the hands of government officials. They set the stage for sacrificing the individual to the mob.

What Would Thomas Jefferson Think About This?

"The moral duties which exist between individual and individual in a state of nature, accompany them into a state of society, and the aggregate of the duties of all the individuals composing the society constitutes the duties of that society towards any other; so that between society and society the same moral duties exist as did between the indviduals composing them, while in an unassociated state, and their maker not having released them from those duties on their forming themselves into a nation."
—Thomas Jefferson,1793

Recommended Reading

Issue #11

Isolationism

Statist Viewpoint
Isolationism is bad.

The Other Side of the Story
In foreign policy, America's founders believed our government should stay neutral but, as private individuals, Americans should travel, trade and be friendly with everyone. Powerseekers call this isolationism. They want the government involved in the affairs of other nations. This leads easily to war, the most exciting use of power.

> *"The great rule of conduct for us, in regard to foreign nations is in extending our commercial relations, to have with them as little political connection as possible."*
>
> —George Washington, 1796

Research the causes of America's entry into the two world wars and you will see the wisdom of the Founders' advice.

What Would Thomas Jefferson Think About This?

"Commerce with all nations, alliance with none, should be our motto."
   —Thomas Jefferson, 1799

"We have a perfect horror at everything like connecting ourselves with the politics of Europe."   —Thomas Jefferson, 1801

"I have ever deemed it fundamental for the United States, never to take active part in the quarrels of Europe. Their political interests are entirely distinct from ours...They are nations of eternal war."
   —Thomas Jefferson, 1823

Recommended Reading & Listening

THE FINAL SECRET OF PEARL HARBOR by Admiral Robert A. Theobald, USN Retired. Published by Devin-Adair, NY, 1954. For ages 14 and up.

"FREE SOCIETIES AND FOREIGN AFFAIRS" in THE LIBERTARIAN ALTERNATIVE by Tibor Machan. (see section IV). Published by Nelson Hall, Chicago. 14+.

"UNITED STATES AT WAR" by Knowledge Products,, Nashville, TN. For ages 14 and up.

THE LIFE AND SELECTED WRITINGS OF THOMAS JEFFERSON, edited by Koch and Peden. See Jefferson's letters about war. Published by Random House, NY, 1972. For ages 15 and up.

Issue #12

Unions Saved Workers

Statist Viewpoint

Businesses refused to grant higher wages or better working conditions to workers until the workers formed unions and forced these changes.

The Other Side of the Story

Unions did not bring better lighting to the factories, Thomas Edison did. A hundred years ago the new systems of scientific management found that workers produced more when they had better lighting, ventilation and other amenities. As soon as these were invented, the more progressive businesses began using them to gain a competitive advantage over the less progressive businesses.

Unions do raise wages, but in so doing they also cause unemployment. An expensive worker is a worker likely to be replaced by a machine or some other innovation. If wages are forced up very much, the firm might even close down or move out of the country.

A worker with a $50,000 hydraulic backhoe can dig more ditches and earn higher wages than one with a $20 shovel. The only way to achieve a real, lasting improvement in wages and working conditions is to accumulate the tools, training, raw materials and other factors necessary for the workers themselves to be more *productive*. Unions have little to do with it, but they take the credit.

The best — some would say the only — real protection for workers is a free market in which employers must bid against each other for labor. Competition. Good workers will have a choice about taking their higher wages in the form of cash or in the form of health plans, pensions or other benefits. Bad workers will have the choice of either earning bad wages or becoming better workers.

Unions have been helpful to workers, this is true. But the help has been exaggerated. If all costs, hidden as well as unhidden, were weighed against benefits, the result would likely not be encouraging.

Recommended Reading

"LABOR, WAGES AND EMPLOYMENT" in FREE MARKET ECONOMICS, A BASIC READER, by Bettina Bien Greaves published by the Foundation for Economic Education. For ages 13 and up.

Issue #13

Social Security is Beneficial

Statist Viewpoint

Social Security is a wonderful example of "social engineering" by government to relieve hardship.

The Other Side of the Story

We don't hear this viewpoint much any more, even the most dedicated statists now realize Social Security is really just a gigantic Ponzi scheme that is impoverishing the young. As such, it is a wonderful example of government's social engineering.

Named after swindler Charles Ponzi, a Ponzi scheme is a pyramid scam like a chain letter. Investors are paid not from their investment's earnings but from the money poured in by new investors. Ponzi schemes are inherently unstable and they eventually go broke.

Recommended Reading

"BURDEN FOR GRANDCHILDREN" in WALL STREET JOURNAL, 9 April, 1991, p. 18. For ages 15 and up.

"GENERATION WAR" in NEWSWEEK, 10 February, 1992, p. 8. For ages 15 and up.

HOW YOU CAN KEEP SOCIAL SECURITY FROM SHATTERING YOUR FAMILY by Richard J. Maybury, Henry-Madison Research, Box 1616-G, Rocklin, CA 95677). For ages 15 and up.

"SIXTYSOMETHING" in U.S. NEWS AND WORLD REPORT, 23 April, 1990, p. 80 and 14 May 1990, p. 82. For ages 15 and up.

"SOCIAL SECURITY" in WALL STREET JOURNAL, 15 January, 1990, p. 1. For ages 15 and up.

Speech by Commissioner of Social Security John A. Svahn, VITAL SPEECHES OF THE DAY, 1 September, 1982. For ages 15 and up.

Issue #14

War

Statist Viewpoint

War is good for the economy.

The Other Side of the Story

Of all the half-truths commonly taught, this must be the most vicious. The economy is not a machine, it is people; killing them is not good for them.

What Would Thomas Jefferson Think About This?

"Never was so much false arithmetic employed on any subject, as that which has been employed to persuade nations that it is in their interest to go to war."

—Thomas Jefferson

Even those who are not killed or wounded usually suffer. Wars bring higher taxes, inflation, shortages, dislocations and massive malinvestment; they are followed by recessions and depressions.

Some persons do benefit. Firms and their employees who make weapons earn more money, but they are only a small part of the population, seldom more than ten percent.

War does tend to reduce unemployment to some extent. Everyone who wants a job can find one, because of the boom caused by inflation of the money supply. Also, some who would otherwise be unemployed are killed.

Government always profits from war. Government emerges from war larger and more powerful. War is generally the most effective way for government to grow.

But on balance for the nation as a whole, war is always a catastrophe. It is the most expensive and destructive thing humans do. Any alternative is cheaper.

This isn't to say we should not defend our homes and families. We should, certainly — if we are sure the threat to our homes and families is real. But the war will not be good for the economy.

Recommended Listening

UNITED STATES AT WAR audiotapes by Knowledge Products (12 two-tape sets, American Revolution through the Vietnam War). Narrated by George C. Scott. For ages 14 and up. Audiotape produced by Knowledge Products, Nashville, TN, distributed by Bluestocking Press, Placerville, CA.

Issue #15

Sacrifice

Statist Viewpoint

Sacrifice means loss, and sacrifice is good, so loss is good and profit is bad.

The Other Side of the Story

When Jesus Christ died on the cross, did he do it for nothing?[6]

He was trying to achieve something he wanted. He was expending something valuable, his life, in hopes of accomplishing something he valued more. He was seeking a gain.

The meaning of the word sacrifice has been changed. Originally sacrifice meant investment. You made an expenditure or took a risk in hopes it would lead to a profit of some kind. In the story of Cain and Abel, sacrifices were made to gain favor with God.

Today sacrifice means doing something without expectation of gain. We are supposed to feel good about doing for others, but feel guilty about doing for ourselves. Movies and

---

[6]My thanks to friend Barry Conner for contributing this insight.

books make heroes of persons who suffer losses, and villains of persons who prosper. The wealthy industrialist has become the all-purpose bad guy.

Part of this change in the meaning of sacrifice is due to the false economic assumption that life is a zero sum game. In a zero sum game, for one person to win another must lose.

In a free market controlled by common law and the forces of competition, both parties in a transaction can earn a profit. (For a more detailed study of this, read Ayn Rand's CAPITALISM: THE UNKNOWN IDEAL.)

Recommended Reading

CAPITALISM: THE UNKNOWN IDEAL BY AYN RAND. Published by New American Library, NY. For ages 15 and up.

CLICHES OF SOCIALISM by the Foundation for Economic Education, Irvington-on-Hudson, NY. For ages 14 and up.

WHATEVER HAPPENED TO JUSTICE? (chapters 10 and 11) by Richard J. Maybury, published by Bluestocking Press, Placerville, CA, 1993.

Issue #16

Their Motives Were Corrupt

Statist Viewpoint

The American Revolution was not about liberty. The founders were corrupt, they launched the revolution to profit from it.

The Other Side of the Story

Many books about American history attempt to discredit the founders by claiming they led the revolution for personal gain.

**What Would
Thomas Jefferson
Think About This?**

"And for the support of this declaration, with a firm reliance on the protection of divine providence, we mutually pledge to each other our lives, our fortunes, and our sacred honor.
—Thomas Jefferson
Declaration of Independence

Three points. First, doing something for personal gain does not make it dishonorable.

Second, when one person gains, this does not mean others must lose. It is entirely possible for one person to do something for personal gain and in the process accomplish ends that benefit many.

Third, the founders risked their lives and some suffered horribly in the revolution exposing themselves to direct enemy fire.

In a small cemetary at Berkeley Plantation on Virginia's James River is a tablet with this inscription:

"By signing the Declaration of Independence, the 56 Americans pledged their lives, their fortunes and their sacred honor.

"It was no idle pledge.

"Nine signers died of wounds during the Revolutionary War.

"Five signers were captured or imprisoned.

"Wives, children were killed, jailed, mistreated or left penniless.

"Twelve signers' houses were burned to the ground.

"Seventeen signers lost everything they owned.

"No signers defected.

"Their honor, like their country, remained intact."

Did they do it for personal gain? Yes, they made the sacrifice in hopes of acquiring a better life for themselves, their families and their country.

Misleading Terms

Watch for these misleading terms:

"Debt to society." Society does not exist, only individuals exist. Take away all the individuals and there is no society. Someone who sets out to pay his debt to "society" usually ends up paying the government.

"Democracy." Democracy is majority rule but it is often used to mean liberty. In reality, democracy is one of the most serious threats to liberty. (See WHATEVER HAPPENED TO JUSTICE? by Richard J. Maybury published by Bluestocking Press.)

"The economy." This term is used by virtually all writers, so you must watch closely to see how it is used. "The economy" is seen by statists and other powerseekers as a kind of machine that can be adjusted or "fine tuned." In reality, the economy is a kind of ecology made of biological organisims—humans. Trying to fine tune or adjust them tends to damage them.

"Germany invaded Poland." We are forever hearing about Germany doing this, Britain doing that, or Russia or the U.S. doing something else. The fact is that specific

German officials do it, as is the case in all nations. All Germans are not involved—many may be completely opposed to the act—and so forth for all nations. By referring to governments as if they were entire nations, we collectivize guilt and and set the stage to punish all the citizens for the actions of a few. This is one of the main causes of war. For a good insight into the ways collectivized guilt prolonged the Second World War read UNCONDITIONAL SURRENDER (published by Rutger's University, out of print—check your library) by historian Anne Armstrong. Armstrong shows that the Allies refused to acknowledge that many Germans hated Hitler and were trying to kill him; when these Germans asked for help, the Allies ignored them. The Allics' assumption that they were fighting "Germany" instead of specific Germans prolonged the war and led to millions of needless deaths. Another excellent book is HITLER'S GERMAN ENEMIES by Louis L. Snyder, published by Hippocrene Books, NY, 1990. This book gives the anti-Hitler German side of the story (for ages 15 and up).

"Patriotism." Suppose the government is harming the country, and you resist. Are you being a traitor, or a patriot?

When the American founders were trying to overthrow their government and establish a new nation, the soldiers sometimes became disheartened by the overwhelming difficulty of the task. In the freezing winter of 1776-77, George Washington ordered that Thomas Paine's new pamphlet THE AMERICAN CRISIS be read to his soldiers. The pamphlet began: "These are the times that try men's souls. The summer soldier and the sunshine patriot will, in this crisis, shrink from the service of his country; but he that stands it now, deserves the love and thanks of man and woman. Tyranny, like hell, is not easily conquered." The government was overthrown, and the new nation established.

Statists sometimes get control of the government and use patriotism as their excuse for doing harm to the country. "Patriotism is the last refuge of a scoundrel," said the great English lexicographer Samuel Johnson.

Sometimes statists are able to rally the nation behind their cause. "When a whole nation is roaring Patriotism at the top of its voice, I am fain[7] to explore the cleanness of its hands and purity of its heart," wrote Ralph Waldo Emerson.

Mark Twain summed up the American view of patriotism: "My kind of loyalty was loyalty to one's country, not to its institutions or its officeholders."

If you remain dedicated to the *principles* on which America was founded, you'll be the kind of patriot Thomas Jefferson and the other founders admired.

"Rights" (also sometimes "Entitlements"). Under the old common law our rights were limited and clearly defined. You had the God-given right to be secure in your life, liberty and property, no one was allowed to encroach. Today we have a "right" to education, a "right" to medical care, a "right" to food, clothing and shelter.

---

[7]compelled.

One person's right is another person's obligation. If I have a right to all these benefits, then someone else is obligated to provide them for me. This someone is, therefore, my slave.

"Social Justice" (also sometimes "Social Equity") This is one of the most cleverly misleading terms in use today. It's so similar to the old common law word "justice" that persons who believe in liberty are easily misled into voting for it, and therefore voting for more statism.

Social justice means using political power to rob Peter to subsidize Paul. Generally statists who speak of social justice are hoping power will be used to "level" society, meaning to take from haves and give to have nots. The scheme always sounds so attractive, especially to have nots, but in the real world it leads inexhorably to higher taxes, more powerful bureaucracies, slower economic development and unemployment.

There's a reason the commandment forbids us to covet our neighbor's goods. And, there's a reason persons who believe in "social justice" so often speak ill of religion.

"Unregulated." This word, although it literally means free, is used by statists as an automatic indictment. Powerseekers believe anything that is unregulated by government is bad. They give no consideration to the fact that common law and the forces of competition are by far the most effective form of regulation, if they are allowed to operate. Government regulation often stifles competition and common law, and creates unfair advantages.

Politics Has Become Religion

When discussing politics, history or economics, bear in mind that many Americans have been unknowingly steeped in statism to the point that government has become their de facto God. It is their source of security and the solution to their problems. They have faith in it.

To challenge their politics is to challenge their religion, which can be emotionally unsettling for them.

Further, it can put you in the position of being a heretic, and heretics are often treated unkindly.

When in the presence of statism, go carefully, these are deep waters.

Positive Indicators

The indicators listed in the following section show that a book agrees with the original American philosophy.

Make notes while the indicators are fresh in your mind. Under each indicator is a space for your own list of books that agree with the indicator. (More of my own favorite books are listed in WHATEVER HAPPENED TO PENNY CANDY? and WHATEVER HAPPENED TO JUSTICE?

Positive Indicator #1

Quality of Life

When a book reveals or discusses the amazing advancement in the quality of life during the past two centuries (since 1776), this is a good sign. This advancement has been due almost entirely to industrial capitalism which was made possible by the common law principles of the American Revolution.

A book that contrasts human life before and after 1776 is rare and wonderful.

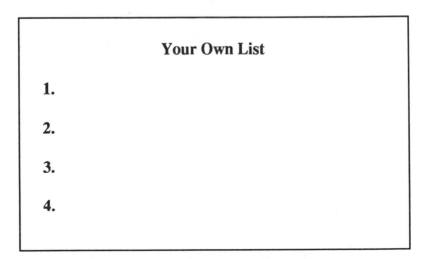

Your Own List

1.

2.

3.

4.

Recommended Reading

CAPITALISM AND THE HISTORIANS edited by F.A. Hayek.
Published by the University of Chicago Press,
1954. For ages 15 and up.

DISCOVERY OF FREEDOM by Rose Wilder Lane. Published by Laissez Faire Books, San Francisco,
California. For ages 14 and up.

GIVE ME LIBERTY by Rose Wilder Lane. Out of print.
For ages 14 and up.

"FACTS ABOUT THE INDUSTRIAL REVOLUTION" by Ludwig
von Mises in FREE MARKET ECONOMICS, A BASIC
READER by Bettina Bien Greaves. Published by
Foundation for Economic Education, Irvington-
on-Hudson, New York. For ages 14 and up.

MAINSPRING OF HUMAN PROGRESS by Henry Grady
Weaver. Published by Foundation for Economic
Education, Irvington-on-Hudson, New York. For
ages 14 and up.

Positive Indicator #2

Individualism

When a book celebrates individualism—independent thinking—or exposes the irrationality of crowds, this is a very hopeful sign.

Your Own List

1.

2.

3.

4.

5.

6.

7.

Recommended Reading and Listening

ATLAS SHRUGGED by Ayn Rand. Published by New American Library, NY. For ages 16 and up.

THE ENTERPRISING AMERICANS by John Chamberlain. Published by Institute for Christian Economics, TX. For ages 15 and up.

ESSAYS ON INDIVIDUALITY edited by Felix Morley. Published by Liberty Press, Indianapolis, 1977. For ages 15 and up.

EXTRAORDINARY POPULAR DELUSIONS AND THE MADNESS OF CROWDS by Charles Mackay. Published by Random House. For ages 15 and up.

THE FEDERALIST PAPERS by Hamilton, Madison and Jay. Published by Mentor Books, NY. For ages 15 and up.

THE FEDERALIST PAPERS. Audiotape produced by Knowledge Products, Nashville, TN, distributed by Bluestocking Press, Placerville, CA. For ages 14 and up.

THE ANTI-FEDERALIST PAPERS AND THE CONSTITUTIONAL CONVENTION DEBATES edited by Ralph Ketcham. Published by Mentor Books, NY. For ages 15 and up.

Positive Indicator #3

Accomplishment Deserves Reward

When a book assumes or, better yet, explicitly teaches, that an individual should be rewarded for his accomplishments, this is a hopeful sign.

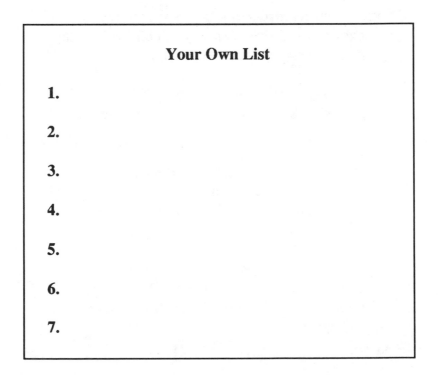

Your Own List

1.

2.

3.

4.

5.

6.

7.

Recommended Reading

CAPITALISM FOR KIDS: GROWING UP TO BE YOUR OWN BOSS by Karl Hess. Published by Enterprise Publishing, Wilmington, DE. Distributed by Bluestocking Press. For ages 9 and up.

DISCOVERY OF FREEDOM by Rose Wilder Lane, published by Laissez Faire Books, San Francisco, CA. For ages 14 and up.

GIVE ME LIBERTY by Rose Wilder Lane, Bluestocking Press, Placerville, CA. For ages 14 and up.

MAINSPRING OF HUMAN PROGRESS by Henry Grady Weaver, published by Foundation for Economic Education, Irvington-on-Hudson, New York. For ages 14 and up.

ROOTS OF CAPITALISM by John Chamberlain. Published by Liberty Press, Indianapolis, 1976. For ages 15 and up.

Positive Indicator #4

Higher Law Exists

A book that assumes there is a "higher law" than any human law will be a rare gem.

Your Own List

1.

2.

3.

4.

5.

6.

7.

8.

Recommended Reading

"THE AMERICAN CONTRIBUTION" in the CONSTITUTION OF LIBERTY by F.A. Hayek (see chapter 12). Published by the University of Chicago Press, 1960. For ages 17 and up.

THE BIBLE or other religous books, depending on your personal belicfs.

THE DRINKING GOURD by F. N. Monjo. Published by Harper Collins, NY. For ages 4-8.

LITTLE TOWN ON THE PRAIRIE (see chapter 8, "Fourth of July") by Laura Ingalls Wilder. Published by Harper Collins, NY. For ages 7 and up.

THE REVOLUTIONARY YEARS, by Mortimer Adler. Published by Encyclopedia Britannica, Chicago, 1976. Out of print. For ages 16 and up.

JONATHAN MAYHEW'S SERMON. Published by Bluestocking Press, Placerville, CA. For ages 14 and up.

Recommended Viewing

JUDGMENT AT NUREMBERG. Spencer Tracy. The Nuremberg trials and the choices judges made.

Positive Indicator #5

Heroes Use Brain Not Brawn

Search for books that have heroes who are resourceful problem solvers rather than action figures. A little violence is probably okay, but the emphasis should be on intelligence not power.

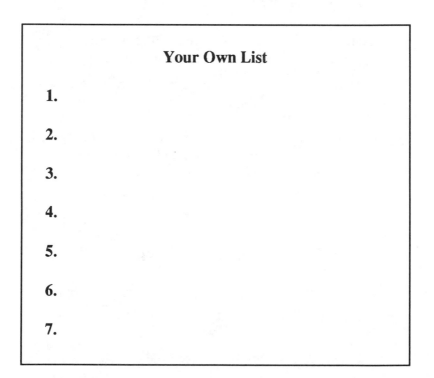

Your Own List

1.

2.

3.

4.

5.

6.

7.

Recommended Reading

AMERICA by Alistair Cooke. Published by Alfred A. Knopf, NY, 1973. For ages 14 and up.

Biographies of Thomas Edison and other inventors and scientists.

CONNECTIONS by James Burke. Published by Little, Brown & Co., Boston, 1978. For ages 14 and up.

THE ENTERPRISING AMERICANS by John Chamberlain. Published by Institute for Christian Economics, TX. For ages 15 and up.

THE HARDY BOYS, TOM SWIFT and NANCY DREW books. Original edition. Published by Applewood Books, MA. For ages 10 and up.

LITTLE HOUSE BOOKS by Laura Ingalls Wilder. Published by Harper Collins, NY. For ages 7 and up.

LUDWIG VON MISES: SCHOLAR, CREATOR, HERO by Murray N. Rothbard. Published by the Ludwig von Mises Institute, Auburn, AL, 1988. For ages 16 and up.

Positive Indicator #6

Evidence vs. Opinion

A book should emphasize the overwhelming importance of rational thought. The reader should be encouraged to seek *evidence* and to examine this evidence logically and dispassionately. A measurement should carry more weight than the opinion of the largest crowd.

Hoaxes abound, and some are astoundingly popular even among learned scholars who ought to know better. Perhaps the most valuable defense you can teach your child is the habit of asking "Where is the evidence?" and to require that this evidence be measurable and verifiable.

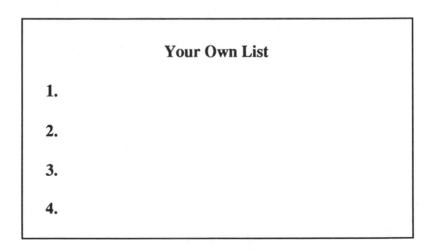

Your Own List

1.

2.

3.

4.

Recommended Reading

ADVENTURES OF SHERLOCK HOLMES (all stories) by Arthur Conan Doyle. Variety of publishers. For ages 13 and up.

CAPITALISM AND THE HISTORIANS edited by F.A. Hayek. Published by University of Chicago Press, 1963. For ages 14 and up.

COSMOS by Carl Sagan. Published by Random House, 1980. For ages 13 and up.

ECONOMICS ON TRIAL by Mark Skousen. Published by Irwin Professional Publishing, Burr Ridge, IL. For ages 16 and up.

STAR TREK stories featuring the characters of Spock or Data. Variety of publishers.

TODAY AND TOMORROW AND... by Isaac Asimov. Published by Dell, NY, 1973. For ages 13 and up.

Positive Indicator #7

Objective Truth

Right and wrong are not matters of opinion. They may be difficult to discover but they do exist and they cannot be made up.

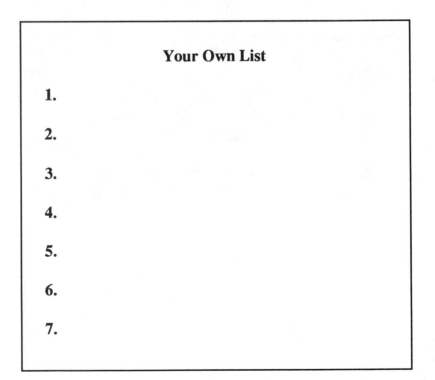

Your Own List

1.

2.

3.

4.

5.

6.

7.

Recommended Reading

THE BIBLE or other religous books, depending on your personal beliefs.

THE CONSTITUTION OF LIBERTY by F.A. Hayek. Published by University of Chicago Press. For ages 16 and up.

LITTLE TOWN ON THE PRAIRIE by Laura Ingalls Wilder. Published by Harper Collins, NY. For ages 7 and up.

ORIGINS OF THE COMMON LAW by Arthur R. Hogue. Published by Liberty Press, Indianapolis, 1966. For ages 16 and up.

PLANNED CHAOS by Ludwig von Mises. Published by the Foundation for Economic Education, Irvington-on-Hudson, NY, 1947. For ages 16 and up.

WHATEVER HAPPENED TO JUSTICE? by Richard J. Maybury published by Bluestocking Press, Placerville, CA. For ages 12 and up.

Positive Indicator #8

TANSTAAFL

When describing benefits of government programs, a book should also give detailed, *quantified* descriptions of all costs and risks, including those that are hidden, and the persons who are bearing these costs and risks. TANSTAAFL: There Ain't No Such Thing As A Free Lunch.

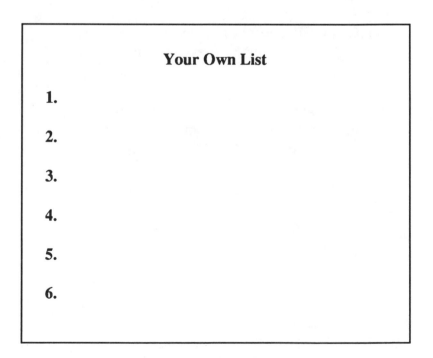

Your Own List

1.

2.

3.

4.

5.

6.

Recommended Reading

"ECONOMIC TEACHING AT THE UNIVERSITIES" in PLANNING FOR FREEDOM by Ludwig von Mises (see Chapter 11). Published by Libertarian Press, South Holland, IL, 1974. For ages 17 and up.

ECONOMICS IN ONE LESSON by Henry Hazlitt, published by Crown, NY. For ages 15 and up.

ECONOMICS ON TRIAL by Mark Skousen. Published by Irwin Professional Publishing, Burr Ridge, IL. For ages 16 and up.

"TANSTAAFL, THE ROMANS AND US," in WHATEVER HAPPENED TO PENNY CANDY? 3rd edition, by Richard J. Maybury. Published by Bluestocking Press, Placerville, CA. For ages 10 and up.

Positive Indicator #9

Overcome Problems
and Move Forward

Perhaps more than anything else, a book should assume humans have the ability to overcome their problems and move forward. Believe it or not, a popular theme in novels today is that all is lost, there is no hope, the individual is helpless.

One of the most noteworthy characteristics of America's founders is that they were aware their own world, and indeed their own characters and personalities, were not the best that humans could do. They worried about slavery, poverty and war, and wanted something better. More importantly, they knew enough law and economics to believe something better was possible and they were working toward this goal.

They were not utopians. They realized a perfect society is not possible. But they knew we could do much better and they were trying to create the legal environment that would enable this to happen.

After the battles of Lexington and Concord, Thomas Paine wrote COMMON sense. This generated support for overthrow of the government and the Declaration of Independence. COMMON sense was probably the most important and popular work ever published in America; George Washington referred to its "sound doctrine and unanswerable reasoning." In it Paine wrote of the revolution and the better world to come.

> 'Tis not the concern of a day, a year, or an age; posterity are virtually involved in the contest and will be more or less affected even to the end of time by the proceedings now. ...
>
> O! ye that love mankind! Ye that dare oppose not only the tyranny but the tyrant, stand forth! Every spot of the Old World is overrun with oppression. Freedom has been hunted round the globe. Asia and Africa have long expelled her. Europe regards her as a stranger, and England has given her warning to depart. O! receive the fugitive, and prepare in time an asylum[8] for mankind."

The belief that a better tomorrow is possible is absolutely essential not only for the rescue of our country but for the mental well-being of the individual. Young people need it desperately.

However, we need to *visualize* this better future, and few of us have imaginations fertile enough to do this alone. We need writers of literature to help us.

This is why I recommend, with parental discretion, the STAR TREK stories. For the most part, STAR TREK is well thought out and places great emphasis on the need for logic and evidence.

---

[8] refuge

The "Prime Directive," which is a centerpiece of the STAR TREK world, is straight from original American principles. All the starship's crewmembers voluntarily take an oath to obey this rule which forbids them to encroach on others.

STAR TREK literature is not of the caliber of Shakespeare or Mark Twain, and issues from specific episodes may be inconsistent with a family's own belief system, but much of it is good, and it provides the hope we need so much. I encourage you to watch with your children. Many episodes can lead to deeper discussions within the family.

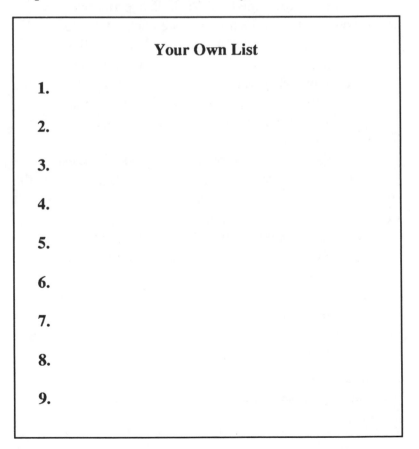

Your Own List

1.

2.

3.

4.

5.

6.

7.

8.

9.

Recommended Reading

THE ENTERPRISING AMERICANS by Chamberlain. Published by Institute for Christian Economics, TX. For ages 15 and up.

EXPLORING THE EARTH AND COSMOS by Isaac Asimov. Published by Crown, NY, 1982. For ages 15 and up.

FREE LAND and LET THE HURRICANE ROAR by Rose Wilder Lane. Distributed by Bluestocking Press, Placerville, CA.

THE GIRL WHO OWNED A CITY by O.T. Nelson. Published by Dell Laurel-Leaf, NY. For ages 10 and up.

ISLAND OF THE BLUE DOLPHINS by Scott O'dell. Published by Bantam Doubleday Dell, NY. For ages 10 and up.

JULIE OF THE WOLVES by Jean Craighead George. Published by Harper Collins, NY. For ages 13 and up.

LITTLE HOUSE BOOKS by Laura Ingalls Wilder. Published by Harper Collins, NY. For ages 7 and up.

ROBINSON CRUSOE by Daniel Defoe. Published by Signet, NY, 1961. For ages 13 and up.

ROUGHING IT and LIFE ON THE MISSISSIPPI by Mark Twain. Bantam, NY, 1960. For ages 14 and up.

WISDOM OF ADAM SMITH by Benjamin Rogge. Published by Liberty Press, Indianapolis, 1976. For ages 15 and up.

YOUNG INDIANA JONES™ published by Random House, NY. For ages 10 and up.

Examples

To get you started reading information consistent with the principles of America's founders, here are three articles written by Richard Maybury that originally appeared in FREE MARKET newsletter published by the Mises Institute and reprinted with permission.[9]

The articles are about American history.

Following these articles is a list of authors whose work is generally consistent with the principles of America's founders.

---

[9]Ludwig von Mises Institute, 325 Pennsylvania Avenue, S.E., Washington, D.C. 20003. Academic offices: Auburn University (205) 826-2500.

The Great Thanksgiving Hoax[10]

By Richard J. Maybury

Each year at this time school children all over America are taught the official Thanksgiving story, and newspapers, radio, TV, and magazines devote vast amounts of time and space to it. It is all very colorful and fascinating.

It is also very deceiving. This official story is nothing like what really happened. It is a fairy tale, a whitewashed and sanitized collection of half-truths which divert attention away from Thanksgiving's real meaning.

The official story has the pilgrims boarding the May-flower, coming to America and establishing the Plymouth colony in the winter of 1620-21. This first winter is hard, and half the colonists die. But the survivors are hard working and tenacious, and they learn new farming techniques from the Indians. The harvest of 1621 is bountiful. The Pilgrims hold a celebration, and give thanks to God. They are grateful for the wonderful new abundant land He has given them.

The official story then has the Pilgrims living more or less happily ever after, each year repeating the first Thanksgiving. Other early colonies also have hard times at first, but they

[10]Reprinted with permission from THE FREE MARKET, November 1985 issue, published by the Ludwig von Mises Institute, 325 Pennsylvania Avenue, S.E., Washington, D.C. 20003. Academic offices: Auburn University (205) 826-2500.

soon prosper and adopt the annual tradition of giving thanks for this prosperous new land called America.

The problem with this official story is that the harvest of 1621 was not bountiful, nor were the colonists hardworking or tenacious. 1621 was a famine year and many of the colonists were lazy thieves.

In his HISTORY OF PLYMOUTH PLANTATION, the governor of the colony, William Bradford, reported that the colonists went hungry for years, because they refused to work in the fields. They preferred instead to steal food. He says the colony was riddled with "corruption," and with "confusion and discontent." The crops were small because "much was stolen both by night and day, before it became scarce eatable."

In the harvest feasts of 1621 and 1622, "all had their hungry bellies filled," but only briefly. The prevailing condition during those years was not the abundance the official story claims, it was famine and death. The first "Thanksgiving" was not so much a celebration as it was the last meal of condemned men.

But in subsequent years something changes. The harvest of 1623 was different. Suddenly, "instead of famine now God gave them plenty," Bradford wrote, "and the face of things was changed, to the rejoicing of the hearts of many, for which they blessed God." Thereafter, he wrote, "any general want or famine hath not been amongst them since to this day." In fact, in 1624, so much food was produced that the colonists were able to begin *exporting* corn.

What happened?

After the poor harvest of 1622, writes Bradford, "they began to think how they might raise as much corn as they could, and obtain a better crop." They began to question their form of economic organization.

This had required that "all profits & benefits that are got by trade, traffic, trucking, working, fishing, or any other means" were to be placed in the common stock of the colony, and that, "all such persons as are of this colony, are to have their meat, drink, apparel, and all provisions out of the common stock." A person was to put into the common stock all he could, and take only what he needed.

This "from each according to his ability, to each according to his need" was an early form of socialism, and it is why the Pilgrims were starving. Bradford writes that "young men that were most able and fit for labor and service" complained about being forced to "spend their time and strength to work for other men's wives and children." Also, "the strong, or man of parts, had no more in division of victuals and clothes, than he that was weak." So the young and strong refused to work and the total amount of food produced was never adequate.

To rectify this situation, in 1623 Bradford abolished socialism. He gave each household a parcel of land and told them they could keep what they produced, or trade it away as they saw fit. In other words, he replaced socialsim with a free market, and that was the end of the famines.

Many early groups of colonists set up socialist states, all with the same terrible results. At Jamestown, established in 1607, out of every shipload of settlers that arrived, less than half would survive their first twelve months in America. Most of the work was being done by only one-fifth of the men, the other four-fifths choosing to be parasites. In the winter of 1609-10, called "The Starving Time," the population fell from five-hundred to sixty.

Then the Jamestown colony was converted to a free market, and the results were every bit as dramatic as those at Plymouth. In 1614, Colony Secretary Ralph Hamor wrote that after the switch there was "plenty of food, which every man by his own industry may easily and doth procure." He said that when the socialist system had prevailed, "we reaped not so much corn from the labors of thirty men as three men have done for themselves now."

Before these free markets were established, the colonists had nothing for which to be thankful. They were in the same situation as Ethiopians are today, and for the same reasons. But after free markets were established, the resulting abundance was so dramatic that annual Thanksgiving celebrations became common throughout the colonies, and in 1863, Thanksgiving became a national holiday.

Thus the real meaning of Thanksgiving, deleted from the official story, is: Socialism does not work; the one and only source of abundance is free markets, and we thank God we live in a country where we can have them.

A Tribute To The
Statue of Ellis Island[11]

by Richard Maybury

(This is a **satire** written in 1986 to give the correct history of the Statue of Liberty.)

December 31, 1999

Today as we enter the 21st Century we should pay tribute to the Statue of Ellis Island. This grand symbol of our government's power and majesty was not always so grand. Only twenty years ago the Lady was a broken, corroded heap of copper and iron. Even her name, Liberty Enlightening the World, was outdated, nearly forgotten, and seriously in need of modernization. The old makes way for the new, it has always been so.

But before we embrace the new—before we enter the next century—let's briefly look back at the long and difficult

---

[11]This article by Richard Maybury originally appeared in THE FREE MARKET, March 1986 issue, published by the Ludwig von Mises Institute, 325 Pennsylvania Avenue, S.E., Washington, D.C. 20003. Academic offices: Auburn University (205) 826-2500. It is reprinted with permission.

journey our nation and this lady have traveled together. We will never pass this way again.

The journey originated in the Middle Ages. During those terrible grim centuries, people were uneducated and they did not yet understand the beauty of political power. Many thought it wrong to have a government empowered to legislate — that is, empowered to make whatever laws appear necessary without regard to moral principles or other idealistic nonsense.

Instead these poor wretches labored under the mistaken assumption that laws should change rarely and only when logically consistent with basic moral principles. A strange legal system called Common Law began to develop.

This ludicrous system was based on the two fundamental laws common to all major religions, philosophies, and other superstitions. These laws were (1) do all you have agreed to do and (2) do not encroach on other persons or their property.

Century after century, Common Law evolved. Government officials knew it was degenerative and they tried to alter or abolish it, but the ignorant common folk clung to their superstitions.

Then during the 1600s shipbuilding technology advanced to the point that many individuals could escape to America, beyond the reach of their government. They hoped to live under Common Law only, without benefit of legislative law.

A curious and greatly misunderstood chain of events then occurred, and these events produced both our country and our Lady.

Since the Common Law changed only slowly, and mostly in ways consistent with the two fundamental laws, the Americans found they were able to *plan ahead* in their work, investment, and trade. Their stable legal environment produced what was known in 1776 as "The System of Natural Liberty." Incorporating what economists call "effective economic calculation," this system was the free market.

For a while the free market seemed to produce considerable abundance for the common people. Poverty declined and America became the most prosperous land ever known.

Then during the 1760s, government officials became concerned about our forefather's contempt for authority. They tried to levy the taxes and regulations that would make Americans accustomed to legislative law.

Our forefathers became angry and violent. The 1776 revolution brought a split from England, and a new nation founded in the principles of Common Law.

Other people around the world saw the abundance of America and assumed this was due to the system of Liberty; they launched their own revolutions. The French were some of the first to revolt, and they did seem to achieve a certain abundance in the wake of this.

Poverty Declined

In gratitude, they donated the statue of Liberty Enlightening the World to America in 1886. This was their way of saying, thank you for teaching us that liberty is the source of prosperity. As the name implied, the upraised torch was the most important part of the statue.

Of course we all know today that the torch is really quite meaningless. Prosperity actually has little to do with Common Law, the system of liberty, or any other such nonsense. It has to do with technological and industrial advancement wrought by enlightened government.

This advancement had lain dormant since the beginning of time, and it just happened to awaken, by coincidence, at the precise moment in history when liberty had awakened. This was an amazing accident, and today thousands of scholars working in government-funded research projects, colleges, and universities have been unable to account for it.

Nevertheless, we all know it was an accident. Advancement comes not from Common Law or the system of liberty, but from dynamic, powerful government. In fact, the archaic Common Law has fallen into such disrepute that it is not even mentioned in schoolbooks.

This is a primary reason the Statue of Ellis Island had to be rebuilt and renamed. It was useless, a broken down structure dedicated to a broken down ideology.

In 1982 a publicity campaign was launched to solicit funds to rebuild not only the physical structure of the statue but also the statue's meaning.

The Lady's original meaning was absent from the deluge of pamphlets, news releases, and TV commercials. Nowhere was there even one line about Common Law. The System of Natural Liberty was not mentioned, nor were, of course, "effective economic calculation" or the free market.

Instead the Ellis Island Foundation accelerated a trend begun in 1903 when Emma Lazarus' poem, "Give me your tired, your poor, etc." was added to the statue. The Lady's connection with her original meaning was severed and she was forevermore linked with immigration.

One pamphlet, for instance, spoke of "the essential unity of the Statue of Liberty and Ellis Island." It first told the story of the immigrants, then explained that this story "reveals the meaning of the Statue of Liberty." A news release explained the statue had become "closely identified with the great flow of immigrants who landed on nearby Ellis Island. . . ."

. . . . The publicity campaign even swathed the statue in a mantle of nationalism, and tied its new meaning to the power of the government. The literature spoke of "the national symbol" and "the most powerful symbol." It praised "the grace and power" of this "national treasure," and of "the national monument."

Today as we move boldly forward into the 21st Century, we have as our most important symbol, the Statue of Ellis Island. May we never forget its new meaning.

The Founding Fathers: Smugglers, Tax Evaders and Traitors?[12]

By Richard J. Maybury

During patriotic holidays, the news media applaud the Founding Fathers. But rarely does anyone mention some important facts about them: that they were smugglers, tax evaders, and traitors.

Not only is this important, it is also praiseworthy; it produced the most advanced civilization ever known.

The Revolution is often said to have begun in 1775 at the Battle of Lexington. In truth, it began in the 16th century when the first colonists began traveling to the New World. Consider the hardships these people faced. Abandoning their relatives and friends, they boarded small leaky boats like the Mayflower — which was only as long as six automobiles — to spend months crossing 3,000 miles of storm-tossed ocean.

Many of these tiny, primitive vessels went down, yet as the years passed, more and more colonists risked their lives to make the journey. IN THE OXFORD HISTORY OF THE AMERICAN

---

[12]Reprinted with permission from THE FREE MARKET, July 1987 issue, published by the Ludwig von Mises Institute, 325 Pennsylvania Avenue, S.E., Washington, D.C. 20003. Academic offices: Auburn University (205) 826-2500.

PEOPLE, historian Samuel Eliot Morison tells us:

> Gottlieb Mittelberger, who came to Philadel-
> phia in 1750, described the misery during his
> voyage: bad drinking water and putrid salt
> meat, excessive heat and crowding, lice so
> thick that they could be scraped off the body,
> sea so rough that hatches were battened down
> and everyone vomited in the foul air; passen-
> gers succumbing to dysentery, scurvy, typhus,
> canker, and mouth-rot. Children under seven,
> he said, rarely survived the voyage, and in his
> ship no fewer than thirty-two died. One vessel
> carrying 400 Palatinate Germans from Rotter-
> dam in August 1738 lost her master and three-
> quarters of the passengers before stranding on
> Block Island after a four-month journey.

Why? What in Europe could have been so horrible that
rational people would risk their lives and their children's lives
to escape it?

Socialism. It wasn't called socialism in those days, but
that is what it was — unlimited government control and
taxation of everything and everybody. There were no free
markets and no free enterprise. Regardless of how honest or
hard working a person was, it did him little good unless he
was in bed with the government.

Out of desperation many rebelled. They evaded the
controls and taxes, creating an underground economy. In
ROOTS OF CAPITALISM, historian John Chamberlain writes that in
France:

For example, it took more than two thousand pages to print the rules established for the textile industry between 1666 and 1730. Weavers had to negotiate with the government for four years in order to obtain permission to introduce "blackwarp" into their fabrics. The effect of the regulations was to freeze French textile production at a certain level, though smuggling and evasion of manufacturing regulations did alleviate the situation somewhat. The violation of the rules often brought terrible penalties: for breaking regulations governing printed calicoes some 16,000 people were either executed or killed in armed brushes with government agents.

America was a vast, uncharted wilderness beyond the reach of the politicians and tax collectors. It was nominally under the control of the European governments, but everyone knew it was too big and too far away for laws to be enforced there.

In short, America was a huge underground economy. Here trade was free and enterprise unrestricted. Taxes were so often evaded that for all practical purposes there were none; a person could keep everything he earned. He could save and invest, and eventually have his own thriving business or farm that would provide jobs for the next wave of immigrants.

Inhabited by rebellious, individualistic smugglers and tax evaders, America quickly became the most prosperous place on earth.

You may have seen pictures of the Pine Tree Flag flown

by American warships during the Revolution. Why would the colonists put a pine tree on their battle flag?

The government had enacted a regulation saying no colonist could cut down tall, straight trees; these trees were to be reserved for masts on Navy ships. This meant the best, most valuable trees on a person's land had, in effect, been confiscated by the government.

When a government tree inspector would come through the forest to select and mark the best trees, colonists would follow him. These inspectors were highly trained experts, good at identifying the best trees for Navy ships — the Navy ships that were constantly pursuing smuggling ships.

When the government's lumberjacks then came through the forest to collect the marked trees, they would find the trees had already been cut and sold — for use on the smuggling ships.

One of these ships was THE LIBERTY, owned by John Hancock. Hancock was a successful wine merchant known throughout the colonies as "The Prince of Smugglers." His reputation eventually earned him the honor of being the first to sign the Declaration of Independence.

Unfortunately, as the story of the Pine Tree illustrates, America did not remain beyond the reach of government. As the colonists' wealth increased, politicians began making more and more efforts to steal — "tax" — this wealth. More and more bureaucrats and troops were sent to the colonies to enforce laws and shut down the underground economy.

The colonists' reaction was dramatic. The infamous Stamp Tax, for instance, was greeted by armed rebellion; tax collectors were tarred and feathered, a procedure which usually resulted in death. When John Hancock was arrested, the people rioted and the government's agents barely escaped with their lives.

This brings us to one of the most important but forgotten events in American history. In his 1818 analysis of the Revolution, John Adams spoke of it when he asked,

> But what do we mean by the American Revolution? Do we mean the American War? The Revolution was effected before the war commenced. The Revolution was in the minds and hearts of the people, a change in their religious sentiments of their duties and obligations.

The key word here is religious. In Adams' analysis, he said a sermon delivered by Reverend Jonathan Mayhew on January 30, 1750, was "read by everybody" and was crucially important in leading to revolution.

In that sermon[13] Mayhew argued that there is a Higher Law than any government's law. The people, he said, are required to obey their government's law only when it is in agreement with Higher Law. Indeed, he argued, if the government violates Higher Law, "we are bound to throw off our allegiance" and "to resist."

What was this Higher Law? — the ancient Common Law which most colonists understood and obeyed faithfully even though they ridiculed and ignored the laws and taxes enacted by politicians.

Common Law had evolved from two basic principles: 1) Do all you have agreed to do, and 2) do not encroach on other persons or their property. These are the two principles on

---

[13]To order a copy of Mayhew's Sermon and John Adams' remarks about it, contact Bluestocking Press, P.O. Box 1014, Dept. EB, Placerville, CA, 95667-1014. Phone: 916-621-1123 or 800-959-8586. FAX: 916-642-9222.

which all major religions and philosophies agree. Each expresses them a bit differently, but all agree on these two laws (and not much else).

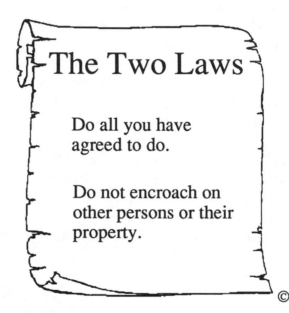

These two laws are the source of all our essential prohibitions against theft, fraud, murder, rape, etc. "Do all you have agreed to do" is the basis of contract law; "do not encroach on other persons or their property" is the basis of criminal and tort law.

Common Law was the law to which the American colonists were dedicated, and it was the law the politicians and bureaucrats were breaking — *they* were encroaching. So the colonists overthrew their government; they committed treason.

This is what the American Revolution was all about — treason. And, this treason was regarded as moral, ethical, and right in every way. It was derived straight from Common Law which was based on the people's religious beliefs. Wrote the great legal scholar Sir William Blackstone, "This law of nature, being coeval with mankind and dictated by God himself, is of course superior in obligation to any other ... no human laws are of any validity if contrary to this."

Contrary to what we so often read, the Americans were not fighting the British. The Americans were British.

The war broke out at Lexington in April 1775, fifteen months before independence was declared. Therefore, for the first fifteen months of the war, America was still a part of Britain and Americans were still Englishmen fighting their own government. As many pamphlets and speeches explained, they were fighting for "The Rights of Englishmen!"

They were enforcing Higher Law. This eternal and immutable law said the politicians and bureaucrats were as human as anyone else and they had no special rights or privileges; they could not encroach on others. "All men are created equal," wrote Thomas Jefferson.

So, the most important and praiseworthy fact about the Founders which is rarely discussed is that they believed in a Higher Law than any government's law, and they did something about it. They evaded their government's taxes and regulations. They delivered speeches and wrote pamphlets informing others, and they eventually overthrew their government and set up a new one more closely in agreement with Higher Law.

The highly advanced, prosperous civilization we now enjoy was the direct result of their enforcement of Higher Law, and this civilization will continue only if Higher Law is re-applied, soon.

Recommended Authors

These authors are not statists. Generally their work is consistent with basic American principles. Many of these persons earn their livings primarily by writing about finance. This forces them to seek principles that reflect reality, for in their industry a mistaken analysis can be immediately costly. Names followed by an asterisk represent non-living authors.

America's Founders
Adams, John*
Adams, Samuel*
Henry, Patrick*
Jefferson, Thomas*
Madison, James*
Paine, Thomas*

Books for Children ages 10 and up
Greaves, Bettina B.
  (economics)
Heinlein, Robert
  (science fiction)
Hess, Karl (liberty & economics)
Lane, Rose Wilder*
  (liberty & westward expansion)
Wilder, Laura Ingalls*
  (liberty & westward expansion)

Economics
Bohm-Bawerk, Eugen von*
Buchanan, James (nobel prize)
Fink, Richard
Friedman, David
Friedman, Milton
Greaves, Bettina B.
Greaves, Percy L.*
Hayek, Frederich A.*
  (nobel prize)
Hazlitt, Henry
Maybury, Richard J.
Mises, Ludwig von*
Rothbard, Murray
Sennholz, Hans F.
Skousen, Mark
Sowell, Thomas
Stigler, George
Webster, Pelatiah
Williams, Walter

Fiction, adult
Rand, Ayn*

Finance
Band, Richard
Bandow, Doug
Browne, Harry
Casey, Douglas
Davidson, James D.
Day, Adrian
North, Gary
Paul, Ron
Pugsley, John

History
Chamberlain, John
Weaver, Henry G.

Law
Bastiat, Frederic*
Blackstone, William*
Maybury, Richard
Spooner, Lysander*

Philosophy
Hospers, John
Lane, Rose Wilder*
Machan, Tibor
Rand, Ayn*
Thoreau, Henry David*

Political
Bergland, David
Block, Walter
Childs, Roy A.
Chodorov, Frank
Harper, F.A.
Hess, Karl
Hummel, Jeffrey R.
Kirzner, Israel M.
Liggio, Leonard
MacBride, Roger
McElroy, Wendy
Mencken, H.L.*
Poirot, Paul L.
Poole, Robert W. Jr.
Read, Leonard*
Reed, Lawrence
Ringer, Robert J.
Samuels, Lawrence K.
Simon, William E.
Smith, George H.

Psychology
Branden, Nathaniel
Szasz, Thomas S.

Science Fiction, adult
Heinlein, Robert
Pournelle, Jerry
Smith, L. Neil

Please Write "Uncle Eric" With Your Ideas, Questions and Concerns

Watch for future books by Richard J. Maybury. One will be answers to questions from readers. Send your questions or comments to him in care of "Uncle Eric," Bluestocking Press, P.O. Box 1014, Dept. EB, Placerville, CA 95667-1014. All letters become property of Bluestocking Press and may be published in whole or in part without payment to the writer. Please tell us if you want your name kept confidential. Topics can include, but are not limited to economics, government, history and law.

If your letter is published in a future "Uncle Eric" book or used in a future "Uncle Eric" audiocassette tape you will receive a free autographed copy of that book or tape.

Mail-Order Book Stores

Write for catalogs from these mail-order book stores that sell books and other resources consistent with the principles of America's founders.

Bluestocking Press, P.O. Box 1014, Dept. EB, Placerville, CA 95667.

Foundation for Economic Education, Irvington-on-Hudson, NY 10533.

Henry-Madison Research, Box 1616-G, Rocklin, CA 95677.

Laissez Faire Books, 942 Howard St., San Francisco, CA 94103.

The Liberator Catalog, Advocates for Self-Government, 3955 Pleasantdale Road #106A, Atlanta, GA 30340.

Liberty Tree Network, 134 98th Avenue, Oakland, CA 94603.

Organizations

- Advocates for Self-Government, 3955 Pleasantdale Road, #106A, Atlanta, GA 30340

- Cato Institute, 224 Second St. SE, Washington, DC 20003

- Contemporary Economics and Business Association (CEBA), P.O. Box 11471, Lynchburg, VA 24506

- Foundation for Economic Education, Irvington-on-Hudson, New York, 10533

- Foundation for Rational Economics and Education, Box 1776, Lake Jackson, TX 77566

- Institute for Humane Studies, George Mason University, 4400 University Drive, Fairfax, VA 22030

- Pacific Research Institute, 177 Post St., San Francisco, CA 94108

- Reason Foundation, 3415 S. Sepulveda Blvd., Ste. 400, Los Angeles, CA 90034

About
Richard J. Maybury
"Uncle Eric"

Richard J. Maybury, also known as "Uncle Eric," is the former Global Affairs editor of Moneyworld, and widely regarded as one of the top free-market writers in America. His articles have appeared in the Wall Street Journal, USA Today and other major publications.

He's been a consultant to business firms in the US and Europe. He is president of Henry-Madison Research.

His books have been endorsed by top business leaders including former U.S. Treasury Secretary William Simon, and he's been interviewed on more than 150 radio and TV shows across America.

He has authored several books in the "Uncle Eric" series and writes an investment newsletter.

He's been around the world, and visited 48 states and 23 countries.

He is a teacher for all ages.

Index

Bluestocking Press

"Uncle Eric" Books byRichard J. Maybury

UNCLE ERIC" TALKS ABOUT PERSONAL, CAREER & FINANCIAL SECURITY. . $ 7.95

WHATEVER HAPPENED TO PENNY CANDY? . . . . $ 9.95

PENNY CANDY TEACHER SUPPORT MATERIAL . . . . $ 0.95

WHATEVER HAPPENED TO JUSTICE? $14.95

ARE YOU LIBERAL? CONSERVATIVE? OR CONFUSED? . . . . $ 9.95

ANCIENT ROME: HOW IT AFFECTS YOUR TODAY . . . . $ 8.95

EVALUATING BOOKS: WHAT WOULD THOMAS JEFFERSON

    THINK ABOUT THIS? . . . . $ 8.95

Uncle Eric's Model (includes seven items above—save 10%) . . $55.95

Reprints

AGREEMENT BETWEEN PARENT & CHILD. . . . . $2.50 postpaid

AGREEMENT BETWEEN TEACHER & STUDENT. . . . . $2.50 postpaid

JONATHAN MAYHEW SERMON / JOHN ADAMS EXPLANATION OF

    THE AMERICAN REVOLUTION. $3.95

Other Bluestocking Press Titles

HOW TO STOCK A HOME LIBRARY INEXPENSIVELY. $14.95

THE HOME SCHOOL MARKET GUIDE . . . . $99.00 postpaid

Order information: Order any of the above from Bluestocking Press (see address below). Payable in U.S. funds. Prices subject to change without notice. If not postpaid, add shipping/handling: $2.50 (U.S.) or $3.50 (Foreign orders, surface) for the first book and $0.75 for each additional book. California residents add sales tax.

Also available
Bluestocking Press Resource Guide & Catalog . . . $3.00 within U.S.

The Bluestocking Press Resource Guide and Catalog lists over 900 items with a concentration in American History, economics and law. It also includes sections on writing, critical thinking, math and the arts. This is a preK through adult level resource guide and catalog, and its history is arranged chronologically by time period. It includes history products as follows: Fiction, nonfiction, primary source material, historical documents, facsimile newspapers, historical music, historical toy-making kits, audio history, coloring books and more. For immediate first class shipping please remit: Cost within U.S.: $3.00. Cost outside U.S.: $3.00 surface shipping or $5.00 air shipping. Payable in U.S. funds.

Bluestocking Press
P.O. Box 1014 • Dept. EB • Placerville • CA • 95667 • USA
Phone orders: 916-621-1123; 800-959-8586 (for MC / Visa orders)

Henry-Madison Research

Richard Maybury writes an investment newsletter about stocks, geopolitics, economics, bonds, currencies, real estate, interest rates, precious metals and more. Much analysis is based on the connection between law and economics. Mr. Maybury gives special attention to events in the former USSR and Mideast, as well as in the U.S.

For a sample copy of Mr. Maybury's newsletter that gives you his latest thinking on important matters that affect you and your money send $5.00 to Henry-Madison Research, Box 1616-G, Rocklin, CA 95677.

For information about Mr. Maybury's lengthy special research reports send a self-addressed stamped business-size envelope to Henry-Madison Research, Box 1616-G, Rocklin, CA 95677.

*"If ever this vast country is brought under a single govern-
ment, it will be one of the most extensive corruptions."*
—Thomas Jefferson, 1822

Thomas Jefferson

"Enemy of Statism"

"Friend of Liberty"

*"I would rather be exposed to the inconveniences attending
too much liberty, than those attending too small a degree of it."*
—Thomas Jefferson, 1791

*"The God who gave us life, gave us liberty at the same time:
the hand of force may destroy, but cannot disjoin them."*
—Thomas Jefferson, 1808

"Remember tanstaafl.
'There Ain't No Such Things As A Free Lunch.'
And spread the word"

—Uncle Eric
quoted from
Whatever Happened to Penny Candy?